Cool as a Cucumber

And Other Expressions about FOOD

BRIDGET HEOS

Illustrated by

AARON BLECHA

Lerner Publications Company

MINNEAPOLIS

Lerner Publications Company
A division of Lerner Publishing Group, Inc.
241 First Avenue North
Minneapolis, MN 55401 U.S.A.

Website address: www.lernerbooks.com

Library of Congress Cataloging-in-Publication Data

Heos, Bridget.
    Cool as a cucumber : and other expressions
  about food / by Bridget Heos.
        p.   cm. — (It's just an expression)
    Includes index.
    ISBN 978–0–7613–7888–4 (lib. bdg. : alk. paper)
    1. English language—Idioms—Juvenile literature.
  2. Food—Juvenile literature. I. Title.
  PE1460.H464 2013
  428.1—dc23   2011044706

Manufactured in the United States of America
1 – PC – 7/15/12

TABLE of CONTENTS

INTRODUCTION

The students in Mrs. Schwarz's class are the **cream of the crop.** In sports, they're no **couch potatoes.** In academics, they **take the cake.** And **in a pickle,** they stay as **cool as a cucumber.**

Right now, they're learning about idioms. <u>Idioms are phrases that mean something different from what they appear to mean.</u> *Take the cake* and the other expressions above are idioms. The students hear idioms every day, in and out of school. They want to know what the story is with these sayings. What do they mean? And how did they come about, anyway?

All sorts of idioms have to do with food. Some sound yummy. Some are disgusting! **Egg on your face?** That's an ugly thing to say—or, rather, an egg-ly thing to say. But what does it mean? In a nutshell…well, read on to learn about these food idioms and more.

SALT of the EARTH

Jake's mom was sick for a few days. A neighbor brought chicken noodle soup. When she left, his mom said, "She's the salt of the earth." Jake could tell it was a compliment. But what did it mean?

Salt of the earth **means "good."** A salt-of-the-earth person does the right thing and helps people.

So how did *salt of the earth* come to mean someone who's kind? Well, salt has always been a valuable spice. It can make many foods tastier. It can also stop food from going bad. Before refrigerators were invented, salt was necessary to help keep meat and other foods from rotting. So it's no wonder that people connect salt with something good!

Where did the "earth" part of the expression come from? To find out, we have to go way back in time to when the Gospels of the Bible were written. In the Bible's Book of Matthew, Jesus tells his followers, "You are the salt of the earth." He meant that he thought his followers were valuable to the whole world. And that's still basically what people mean when they use this expression about someone.

Salt appears in other idioms too. *Worth your salt* means "to be a good worker." In Roman times, soldiers were paid an allowance to buy salt. This was called their *salarium*. The modern English word for a yearly wage, *salary*, comes from this word.

EGG on YOUR FACE

Ethan bragged to his classmates that he could get an A in math without studying. When he failed the test, he was left with egg on his face.

Did a classmate throw eggs at him? No! **Getting egg on your face means that you embarrassed yourself.** You said or did something that made you look foolish.

The saying may come from vaudeville. Vaudeville is a type of live variety show that was popular from the late 1800s to the early 1900s. Performers sang, danced, and acted in skits. If the audience didn't like an act, sometimes they threw eggs. So some unlucky performers ended up with egg on their faces.

This vaudeville performer balances teacups on his head while his assistant looks on anxiously. If an audience didn't like his act, they might have thrown eggs at the performer.

The phrase first appeared in print in the mid-1900s, after vaudeville stopped being popular. But people were still familiar with the tradition.

Another theory is that being left with egg on your face means you didn't wash your face after eating. So food is left on your face. How embarrassing!

Eggs appear in many idioms. A "bad egg" is a rotten person. A "good egg" is the opposite. To *lay an egg* means "to perform badly." "Goose egg" is a saying that means you didn't get any points in a sport or some other activity. It came about because a goose egg is shaped like a zero.

BRING HOME the BACON

For homework, Nevaeh had to read an article in the newspaper. One headline read, "More Women Are Bringing Home the Bacon." Nevaeh loved bacon, so she started reading. But the article wasn't about bacon at all.

Bring home the bacon means "to make money for your family." The article was about the recession (economic slowdown) that hit the United States around 2008. More men than women lost their jobs. Therefore, many women had started bringing home the bacon by themselves.

How did this phrase get started? One theory is that it refers to a contest at county fairs. If you could catch a greased pig, you could bring that piggy home. And bacon, of course, is made from pigs—so you'd be bringing home the bacon.

Or the phrase may refer to an old story. In the 1100s, a wealthy man in Dunmow, England, offered a side of pork, or bacon, to any couple who could prove they had a blissful marriage. They did this by kneeling at the door of the town's church and swearing they had not been unhappy in the last year and a day of their marriage.

Many historians claim there's no way the expression goes back to the 1100s. They believe the saying has to do with a telegram that U.S. boxer Joe Gans *(right)* got from his mother before a big match in 1906. She told him to "bring back the bacon"—which was her way of telling him to bring back the prize. But why would she connect bacon with a prize if this expression didn't already exist? It may have just been because many people like bacon, so she naturally connected bacon with winning. (In fact, Gans *did* win the match. And after winning, he replied with a message saying he was "bringing home the bacon with lots of gravy on it.")

The PEANUT GALLERY

JaVontra's team was up to bat. It was a close game. Fans in the bleachers were yelling, "Don't swing at that!" and "Swing faster!" and "You're too close to the plate!"

The coach said, "Don't listen to the peanut gallery. Listen to me!" JaVontra stared at a bag of peanuts on the bench. What was Coach talking about? **Peanut gallery means "people with an amateur (not expert) viewpoint."** In a baseball game, the coach is the expert. The fans, as a group, are not. A peanut gallery can refer to fans of any sport as well as people with opinions about politics, current events, or anything else.

Originally, the term referred to theater audiences. The upper balcony in the theater was called the gallery. Peanuts were a popular snack.

They were also a popular thing to throw at the stage! In the 1800s, people in the gallery crowd would often do that when they were unhappy with the performance. <u>So the gallery became known as the peanut gallery.</u>

Later, a TV program called the *Howdy Doody Show* brought back the phrase. This children's show, which ran from 1947 to 1960, had a live audience of kids. They sat in what was called the peanut gallery. Sometimes, they sang along or answered questions. But to keep the young audience from getting too loud, the host, Buffalo Bob, would sometimes say, "No comments from the peanut gallery!"

Buffalo Bob Smith poses for a photo with Howdy Doody, a marionette (puppet). During the *Howdy Doody Show*, kids sat in sections of bleachers onstage called the peanut gallery.

COUCH POTATO

Joe had looked forward to relaxing this summer. He watched a lot of TV. But by July, his mom was calling him a couch potato. Was Joe *really* turning into a potato?

Of course not. **A couch potato is somebody who sits around a lot.** It especially refers to someone who is sitting on the couch watching TV all the time.

The phrase first appeared in 1979 in the *Los Angeles Times*. But it has its root in an older phrase. When TV first became popular, it was sometimes called the boob tube. *Tube* referred to

Teenagers gather around the boob tube to watch a Western in the 1950s.

the cathode-ray tube in old TV sets. *Boob* was a word for a silly person. (TV then suffered the same criticism as it does in modern times: that it's mindless entertainment.) Someone who watched lots of TV was a boob tuber.

Enter the potato. A potato *is* a tuber. (A tuber is the thick stem or root on a plant.) Instead of being boob tubers, soon people who watched too much TV were known as couch potatoes. These days, people who spend a ton of time on the computer or playing video games might be known as couch potatoes too.

Dirt clings to potato tubers.

IN a PICKLE

James asked Francesca to go with him to the school play on Saturday. But he forgot that Saturday is his brother's birthday. James is supposed to stay home for the party. He's in a pickle!

What does it mean to be in a pickle? It just means that you're in a difficult situation.

The phrase dates at least to the early 1600s. In *The Tempest,* a play by William Shakespeare, a character asks, "How camest thou in this pickle?" Shakespeare probably used *pickle* not to mean the crunchy green spears but rather the juice they floated in. Made mainly of vinegar, pickle juice is what makes pickles pickles. To create pickles,

These cucumbers sit in vinegar. They will turn into pickles.

people put a cucumber into the juice. The juice soaks into the cucumber and turns it into a pickle—a crisp green veggie with a dill flavor.

Pickle juice was also used to help preserve dead bodies. Gross but true! If a soldier was killed in war, his body was sent home in a barrel filled with pickle juice. The juice helped keep the body from rotting. _So if you were in a pickle—well, it meant that you were dead!_

Luckily, James's situation isn't so dire. Maybe he should eat a pickle and think things over! He could always invite Francesca to come to the party after the play.

In baseball, a runner is in a pickle when he's caught between two bases. He could be tagged out at either one!

APPLE of MY EYE

Kayla's granddad lived out of town. He wasn't big on texting, so they wrote letters. In every letter, he started with, "To the Apple of my Eye." Kayla had heard the phrase in a song. She knew that it meant someone you loved. But she couldn't figure out why. What could apples and eyes possibly have to do with each other?

Long ago, the pupil of the eye was called the apple. It was believed to be a solid sphere. Really, the pupil is an opening that lets light into the part of the eye called the retina. People didn't know that. But they knew that the pupil was important to sight. Sight was precious. *Apple of my eye* **means "something precious."**

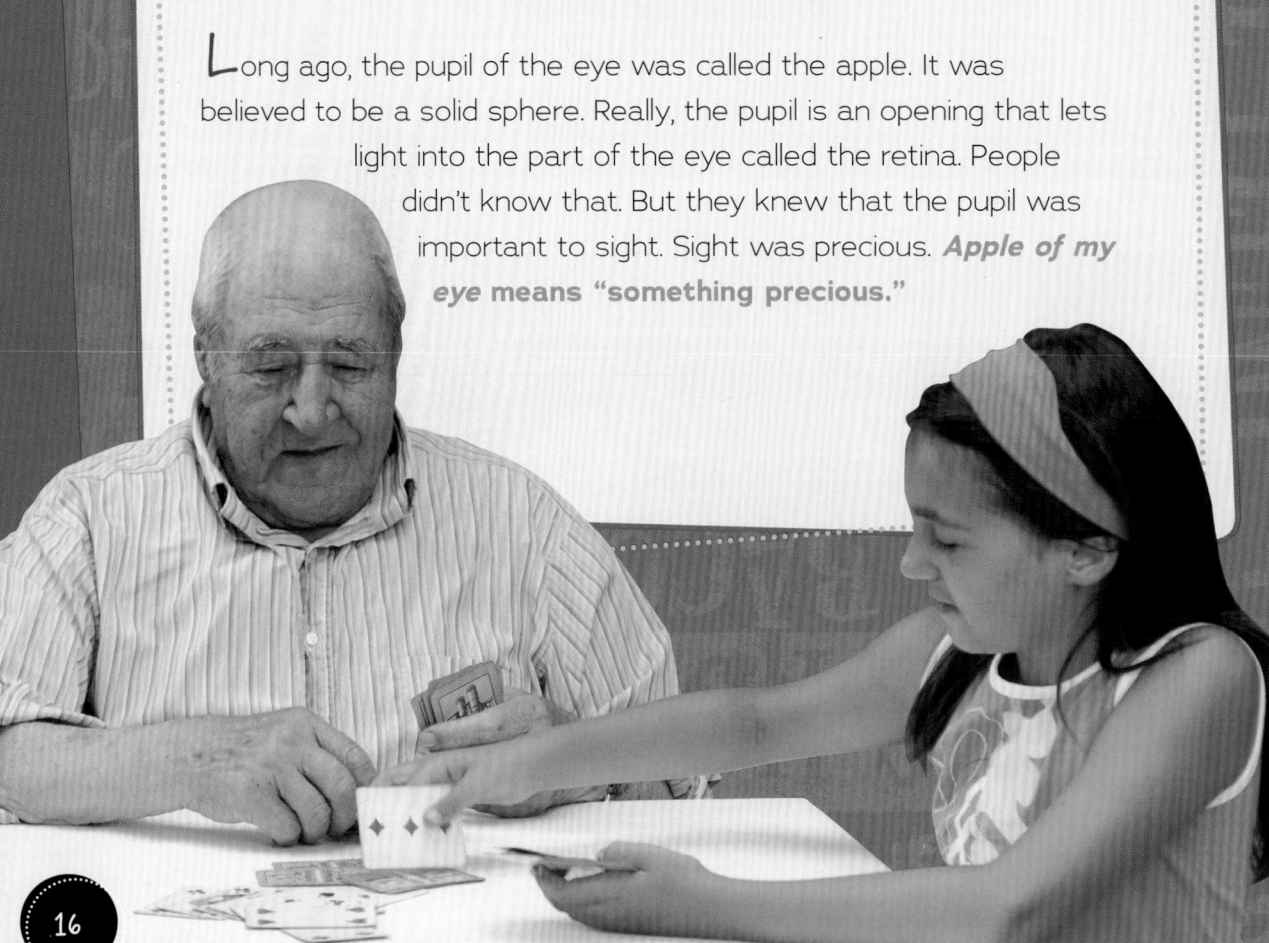

The expression is very old. King Alfred of England recorded it in the 800s. It also appears in English translations of the Bible dating to the 1600s. The Book of Deuteronomy says that God cared for the Israelites, "guarding them as the apple of his eye."

Apple of my eye often describes a parent's or a grandparent's love for a child.

However, it can also describe how a boyfriend feels about a girlfriend or vice versa. In "Sweet Pea," a song by Amos Lee, the singer assures his girlfriend that she is both his sweet pea (a colorful and sweet-smelling flower) and the apple of his eye.

A bouquet of sweet pea flowers would brighten the day for the apple of your eye!

PEACHES and CREAM

Samantha wanted to get a spring ski pass with her friends. Her mom said they couldn't afford it. Sam's mom had been out of work. But she'd gotten a new job. Didn't they have money now?

"We're still paying off bills," her mom said. "Don't worry. In another year, everything will be peaches and cream." What does Sam's mom mean by that?

Peaches and cream means "perfect and good." Why? Well, people have eaten peaches and whipped cream as a yummy treat for a long time. The 1800s was a time when many U.S. workers were struggling to feed their families.

Affording new clothing will be easier once things are back to "peaches and cream" for this family.

Labor leaders promised workers that if they stood up for themselves and fought for better wages, then "we'll all eat peaches and cream." That's how this expression got its start.

Peaches and cream can also refer to a lady's complexion (the coloring of her face). It means a creamy skin tone with a peachy pink glow on the cheeks. Usually, women with blonde or red hair and the pale skin that goes with it are said to have peaches-and-cream complexions.

Taylor Swift has a peaches-and-cream complexion.

COOL as a CUCUMBER

Today Libby's class is giving speeches. Many students are nervous. Gage blushes while he gives his speech. Izzy drops her note cards. But Libby is as cool as a cucumber.

It's not because of a chilly breeze. And no, Libby is not turning into a vegetable! Rather, Libby doesn't feel nervous. *Cool as a cucumber* means "poised and unshaken."

This student looks comfortable making her presentation to the class. She is as cool as a cucumber.

This phrase was used as early as 1615. Around that time, the saying turned up in the popular play *Cupid's Revenge* by Francis Beaumont and John Fletcher. Beaumont and Fletcher call some characters in their play "cold as cucumbers." Why did they think of cucumbers as cold? It's probably because these veggies are made mostly of water. Water carries heat away from your skin or teeth more quickly than air does, so cucumbers feel cool to the touch. *Cool* can also be a way of saying that someone's calm. And just like that, an expression was born!

Maybe Libby can teach her classmates how to calm their nerves on speech day. Then when they give their talks, they won't be beet red—blushing as red as the skin of a beet. Instead, everybody can be cool as cucumbers.

RED HERRING

Rose was watching a mystery with her dad. She said, "I think the neighbor did it." Her dad said, "No, the neighbor is a red herring." Why was her dad talking about fish?

A **red herring is a distraction from the truth.** Mystery writers use red herrings to throw people off track. The old cartoon *A Pup Named Scooby-Doo* even had a character *named* Red Herring! The other *Scooby-Doo* characters often accused him of committing whatever crime they were investigating because he's a bully. But Red Herring was almost always innocent.

So why does *red herring* refer to a distraction from the truth? Well, hunters used this smelly fish to train their hunting animals. On fox hunts, hounds sniff out foxes, and hunters follow the dogs on horseback. So in practice runs, hunters would drag a dead

Despite its strong smell, red herring is a common part of a traditional Danish lunch.

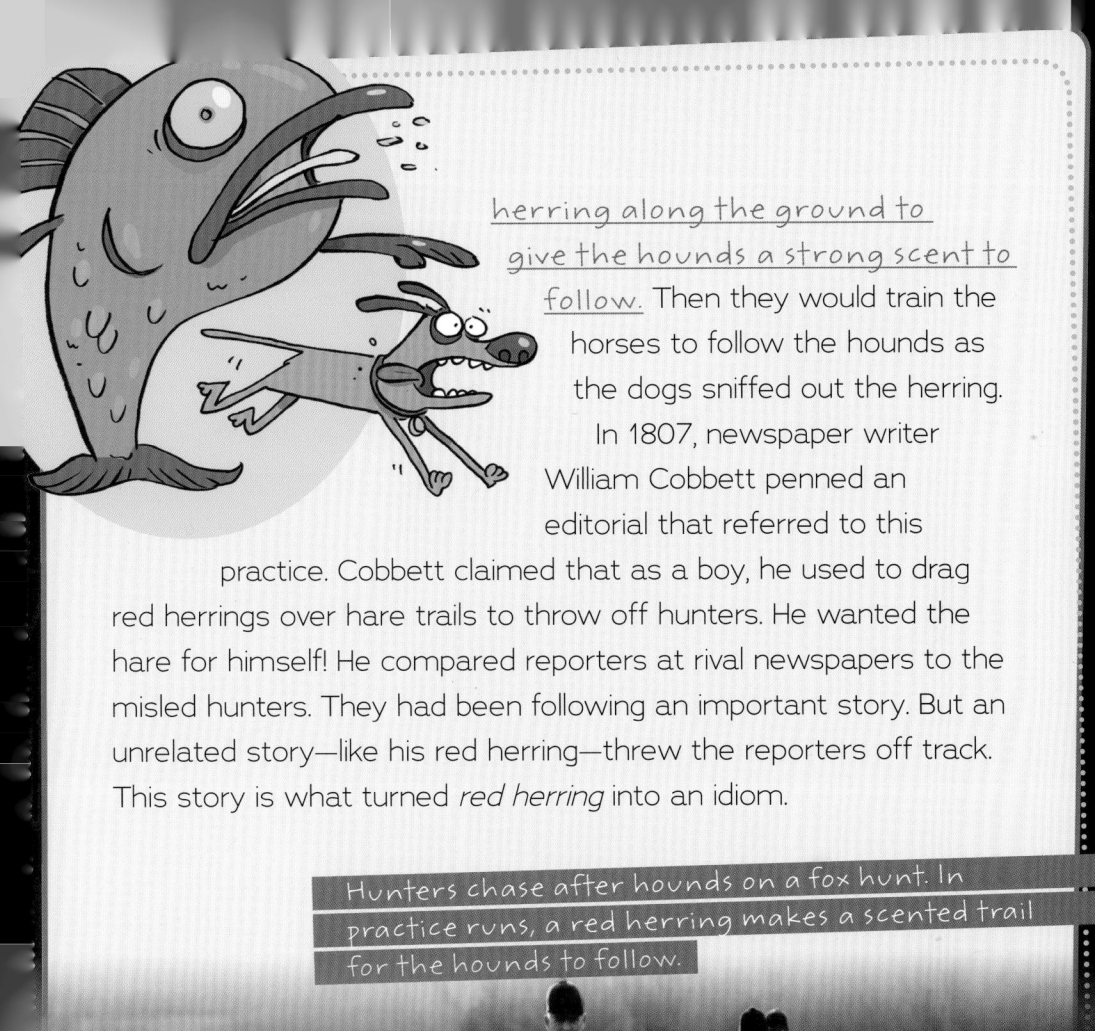

<u>herring along the ground to give the hounds a strong scent to follow.</u> Then they would train the horses to follow the hounds as the dogs sniffed out the herring. In 1807, newspaper writer William Cobbett penned an editorial that referred to this practice. Cobbett claimed that as a boy, he used to drag red herrings over hare trails to throw off hunters. He wanted the hare for himself! He compared reporters at rival newspapers to the misled hunters. They had been following an important story. But an unrelated story—like his red herring—threw the reporters off track. This story is what turned *red herring* into an idiom.

Hunters chase after hounds on a fox hunt. In practice runs, a red herring makes a scented trail for the hounds to follow.

GRAVY TRAIN

Topher mowed lawns to make money in the summer. Mowing five lawns a day in the heat was hard work. Meanwhile, his friend Jake babysat the neighbor's dogs. He walked them twice a day.

The rest of the time, who knows what he did? He probably watched TV in the air-conditioned house with the dogs. "You're riding the gravy train with that job!" Topher told Jake.

This boy gets to sit indoors playing video games for most of his job. He is riding the gravy train!

What did Topher mean? Well, **gravy train means "an easy way to make money or earn a living."** In the early 1900s, *gravy* was slang for easy money. Railroad workers may have called easy trips with good pay "riding the gravy train." That's probably where this expression comes from.

Sometimes people use the phrase *gravy boat* to mean the same thing. A gravy boat is a dish to hold gravy. If Topher can't find a gravy train, maybe he could ride the gravy boat. Or maybe he'll see if *he* can babysit the neighbor's dogs next summer! He might find that the job is not as easy as it looks.

TAKE the CAKE

Maryah's soccer team, the Strikers, lost their first ten games. Other teams started calling them the Striker Outers. That made them get serious.

They practiced extra hard. They started winning. The next season, they won the championship. Maryah overheard another coach say, "The Striker Outers winning it all? That takes the cake!"

Cake would be nice. But winning the championship was better! *Take the cake* means "to win or to top all others." *That takes the cake* refers to something impressive and unexpected.

Cakes have been prizes throughout history. But the expression probably comes from African American dance contests in the 1800s. Side by side, partners did a dancing walk. They were judged, and the prize was a cake. So the winners would literally take the cake.

So why is *that takes the cake* used with something unexpected? Over time, people probably began using it to mean not only the best but whatever is the most amusing, hard to believe, or surprising. Take the Cake and That Takes the Cake are also popular names for a bakery. And that's exactly where Maryah and her team were headed to celebrate their victory!

The dance contests known as cakewalks inspired new styles of music. This sheet music hit stores in 1915.

KERRY MILLS CAKE WALK

MR. MILLS IS THE ORIGINATOR OF THE CAKE WALK.

YOU UNDOUBTEDLY RECALL HIS FAMOUS COMPOSITIONS : "THE GEORGIA CAMPMEETING", "WHISTLING RUFUS" "RASTUS ON PARADE"

F.A. MILLS

PIE in the SKY

Tia is running for student council. Her friend Ian thinks she's making a pie-in-the-sky promise on her campaign poster.

But her poster doesn't say that students can eat pie in the sky. It says they can eat pie in the lunchroom. All day! Every Friday! If elected, Tia will make Friday "Pie Day." No lunch. Just pie.

That's a pie-in-the-sky promise. The school would never allow it. *Pie in the sky* **means "impossible."**

Students deserve real pie, Tia, not pie in the sky! But who made up this expression? Joe Hill. In the early 1900s, he wrote songs for a workers' union (a group that acts together to get fair pay and work conditions). Many workers were paid poorly

and didn't have enough to eat. Coming together, the workers could fight for better wages.

Joe didn't like songs that said you could be happy only in heaven. He thought people could be happy on Earth—if they weren't hungry! In 1911, he wrote a parody, or silly version, of the song "In the Sweet By and By." His song said, "Work and pray. Live on hay. You'll get pie in the sky when you die."

At the time, pie in the sky meant joy in heaven but sadness on Earth. Later, it came to mean "impossible." In the 1950s, the song "High Hopes," sung by Frank Sinatra, offered a new meaning. That song said that you can achieve "high apple pie in the sky hopes."

So maybe Tia will achieve Friday Pie Day after all!

Frank Sinatra's song "High Hopes" told people to have faith in "pie in the sky" ideas.

Glossary

complexion: the coloring of a person's face, including its tone, healthiness, moisture, and texture

fox hunt: a sport in which hunters on horseback follow hounds who follow the scent of a fox

herring: a type of fish. When smoked, it is sometimes called red herring.

idiom: a commonly used expression or phrase that means something different from what it appears to mean

pupil: the black circle appearing at the center of the eye. It is the opening that lets light into the eye so that sight is possible.

recession: a downward turn in business activity, with more unemployment than usual

salary: the payment that a worker earns in a year for doing his or her job

telegram: a written message sent through a telegraph system. Telegraphs encode messages in electric signals sent over wires from one telegraph machine to another.

tuber: the thick stem or root of a plant

union: an organization of workers acting together to get fair pay and working conditions

Further Reading

Cleary, Brian P. *Skin Like Milk, Hair of Silk: What Are Similes and Metaphors?*
Minneapolis: Millbrook Press, 2009.
Bright illustrations and rhyming text explore similes and metaphors, which are
often used in idioms. Learn how to spot these language tricks.

Donovan, Sandy. *Until the Cows Come Home: And Other Expressions about
Animals*. Minneapolis: Lerner Publications Company, 2013.
Check out this book for explanations of idioms involving cows and other animals,
with more comical illustrations from Aaron Blecha.

Dubosarsky, Ursula. *The Word Snoop*. New York: Dial Books, 2009.
Want more of the backstory on English? This book explores clichés, Pig Latin,
similes, and other fun features of our language.

Idiom Site
http://www.idiomsite.com
Search this alphabetical list of idioms for quick and easy definitions.

Moses, Will. *Raining Cats and Dogs*. New York: Philomel, 2008.
This picture book gives short explanations of idioms with the help of funny
illustrations.

"Paint by Idioms"
http://www.funbrain.com/funbrain/idioms
Take the multiple-choice quizzes on this site to test your knowledge of common
idioms from FunBrain.

Terban, Marvin. *Mad as a Wet Hen! And Other Funny Idioms*. Boston: Sandpiper,
2007.
Terban gives the meaning of more than one hundred expressions and provides the
history for many of them.

———. *Scholastic Dictionary of Idioms (Revised)*. New York: Scholastic, 2006.
Terban explains the meaning and history of hundreds of expressions.

World Wide Words
http://www.worldwidewords.org
Word scholar Michael Quinion writes articles and answers questions about words
and expressions.

Index

Photo Acknowledgments

The images in this book are used with the permission of: © Viktorfischer/Dreamstime. com, p. 5 (top); © allesalltag/Alamy, p. 5 (bottom); © Alexey Suprun/Dreamstime.com, p. 6 (top); © Susanna Price/Dorling Kindersley/Getty Images, p. 6 (bottom); © Keystone-France/Gamma-Keystone via Getty Images, p. 7; © Joseph Gough/Dreamstime.com, p. 8 (top); © db2stock/Blend Images/Getty Images, p. 8 (bottom); © UK History/Alamy, p. 9; © Monkey Business Images/Shutterstock.com, p. 10, Courtesy Everett Collection, p. 11; © Huntley Paton/Flickr/Getty Images, p. 12; © Lambert/Archive Photos/Getty Images, p. 13 (top); © Eric Brasseur/Photonica/Getty Images, p. 13 (bottom); © Olle Akerstrom/CORBIS, p. 14; © Paul Spinelli/MLB Photos via Getty Images, p. 15; © Francesco Carta fotografo/Flickr/Getty Images, p. 16; © Anthony Shaw/Dreamstime.com, p. 17 (top); © Elena Elisseeva/Dreamstime.com, p. 17 (bottom); © Spencer Grant/Photolibrary/ Getty Images, p. 18; © Brand X Pictures/Getty Images, p. 19 (top); © Steve Granitz/ Wire Images/Getty Images, p. 19 (bottom); © Milesdavies/Dreamstime.com, p. 20 (top); © Anderson Ross/Photodisc/Getty Images, p. 20 (bottom); Henrik Stenberg/Visit Denmark/Newscom, p. 22; © Travel Ink/Gallo Images/Getty Images, p. 23; © Hill Street Studios/Blend Images/Getty Images, p. 24; © Gyorgy/Dreamstime.com, p. 25 (top); © Brian Leatart/Foodpix/Getty Images, p. 25 (bottom); © Paulburns/Dreamstime.com, p. 26 (top); © moodboard/Cultura/Getty Images, p. 26 (bottom); © Pictorial Press Ltd/ Alamy, p. 27; © Matt Antonino/Dreamstime.com, p. 28 (top); © Dirk Anschutz/Stone/ Getty Images, p. 28 (bottom); © CBS Photo Archive/Getty Images, p. 29.

Front cover: © Todd Strand/Independent Picture Service; © Marilyn Gould/Dreamstime .com (fan).

Main body text set in Adrianna Light 11/17.
Typeface provided by Chank.